W9-AGH-652

Healthy Eating

Claire Llewellyn

QEB Publishing

Copyright © QEB Publishing 2006

First published in the United States in 2006 by
QEB Publishing, Inc.
23062 La Cadena Drive
Laguna Hills, CA 92653
www.qeb-publishing.com

Library of Congress Control Number: 2005911013

ISBN 978-1-59566-192-0

Written by Claire Llewellyn
Designed by Susi Martin
Editor Louisa Somerville
Consultant Ruth Miller B.Sc., M.I.Biol., C.Biol.
Illustrations John Haslam
Photographs Michael Wicks

Printed and bound in China

Picture credits

Getty images Elyse Lewin p20

Words in **bold** are explained

in the glossary on page 22.

Contents

Food, glorious food!

We all need food to stay alive and stay **healthy**. If we didn't eat, our bodies would stop growing and we wouldn't have the energy to move around.

Star tip

Our bodies need lots of different foods. Eating too much of one thing, such as candy or potato chips, can be bad for you.

Without food and water, your body would s-l-o-w d-o-w-n and stop!

 **Do it!**

The food and drink we eat is called our **diet**. Write down everything that you have eaten and drunk in the last two days. Did you eat lots of different foods—or mostly the same?

A little of everything

Imagine being a sheep and eating grass all day long! Our diet contains different foods to give us what we need to grow, keep **active,** and stay healthy. This is called a **balanced diet**.

Star tip

Eat different kinds of foods at every meal. Then you'll be eating a balanced diet.

Fish, meat, cheese, and eggs help our bodies to grow.

Fruit and vegetables help to keep us healthy.

Bread, pasta, and potatoes give us the energy to be active.

Salad sandwich

Make it!

Ask an adult to help you to make a balanced meal. Pile some tuna or grated cheese onto brown bread or pitta and add some crunchy salad. Finish with fruit or yogurt and a drink of fruit juice or milk. Delicious and healthy!

Fruit and vegetables

We need to eat lots of fruit and vegetables. They contain **vitamins**, which help us grow and keep us healthy.

Which fruit and vegetables do you like best?

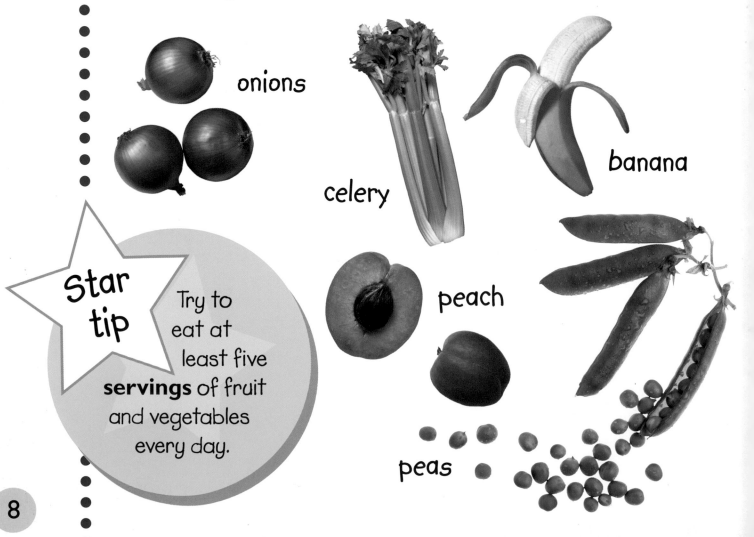

onions

celery

banana

peach

peas

Star tip

Try to eat at least five **servings** of fruit and vegetables every day.

Bite into a crisp apple and a stick of celery. How do they smell and taste? Which other fruit and vegetables can you eat raw?

Make it!

Fruit kebab

Why not make a fruit kebab! Ask an adult to cut up different-colored fruits and then you can thread them one piece at a time onto a toothpick.

Which fruits need to be peeled or sliced? How do they look, taste, and smell?

Energy foods

Every day we need to eat foods that give us energy. Foods such as bread, rice, pasta, and potatoes give us the most energy.

pasta

bread

potatoes

rice

We need these foods so we can run, jump, skip, and swim. Being active is good for our bodies.

Try whole-wheat bread. It takes longer to digest, so you don't feel hungry again so quickly.

Mmmm... yum!

Make it!

Baked potato

1. Clean a big potato and ask an adult to bake it in the oven until it is soft.

2. When it is cooked, ask the adult to cut it in half for you, because it will be very hot.

3. Fill it with one of these foods.

What other fillings could you use?

Next time try a sweet potato. They're delicious!

cheese

sour cream

tuna

You're sweet enough

We can get energy from sugary foods. Fizzy drinks, cookies, candy, and ice cream all contain sugar. But if you eat too much sugar, your diet won't be balanced.

Do it!

Compare a fizzy orange soda with fresh orange juice. The fizzy soda is so sugary that it will make the fresh juice taste quite sharp.

Eating lots of sugary foods is very bad for your teeth. They could **decay**.

Sugar swap

One or two days a week, switch a sweet snack for something healthier.

Which of these would you choose?

yogurt

dried banana

apple

dried fruits and nuts

Fruit smoothie

Make it!

A fruit smoothie is a treat you can enjoy that does not have a lot of added sugar. Choose a banana, some strawberries, or peaches. Ask an adult to blend them in a **blender** with some low-fat yogurt or milk. Add an ice cube for extra-cold froth.

Healthy snacks

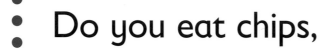

Do you eat chips, peanuts, sausage, and other salty, fatty foods often?

Do it!

The next time you have sausage, ask an adult to broil or bake it instead of frying it. That way, you eat less fat!

If you eat too many of these foods too often, you'll have an unhealthy diet.

It's better to eat them as treats now and then.

plain popcorn

unsalted peanuts

breadsticks

Star tip

The next time you want a bag of chips, try one of these snacks instead.

Make it!

Stick 'n' dip

Make a low-salt snack. Ask an adult to peel and pit an avocado and then blend it in a blender with plain yogurt and lemon juice.

Now ask an adult to chop carrots, celery, and red peppers into bite-size sticks. Scoop up your avocado dip with the healthy dippers.

Drink up!

We should drink at least a quart or two of **fluid** each day to keep our bodies working well.

Try to drink at least a glass of water, milk, or fruit juice at every meal.

Don't forget to drink plenty!

Sip it, slurp it, gulp it! Drink six to eight glasses of fluid a day. Your body needs more when the weather is hot or when you have been very active.

Fruity fizz

Make it!

Make a fruity, fizzy drink.

Put some ice cubes in a glass, then pour in a little of your favorite juice.

Fill up the glass with club soda.

Try other fruit juices, too!

How much food?

We should only eat the amount of food our bodies need.

Most of us need three balanced meals, one or two healthy snacks, and lots of water each day.

If you're small or **inactive**, you won't need as much food as someone who is BIG or very active.

Star tip

Even while you are asleep, your body uses up energy. To give you the energy to get going in the morning, always eat a good breakfast.

oats

fruit and
vegetables

bread, cereals
and potatoes

To stay healthy, your
body needs more
fruit, vegetables,
cereals, and
bread than fat,
sugar, and meat.

milk and
dairy

meat, fish
and eggs

fats and sugars

Do it!

Make a big poster showing
all the food that you eat in
one day. Count up all the
fruit and vegetables on
your poster. Are there five
or more? Did you eat
something from each of the
sections in the chart above?

What's cooking?

Have a go at cooking! You can see how the food you eat is cooked if you help in the kitchen at home.

An adult must help you to use the stove and handle hot things, but there are lots of things you can make by yourself.

Do it!

Ask an adult to help you choose a **recipe** from a cookbook or magazine. Then go shopping together for the things you need. Follow the recipe and make the dish.

Now try it out on your family or friends.

roasted squash
— delicious and sweet

peanuts
— fresh
and nutty

Star tip

Try eating something new and healthy. Have you tried any of these foods?

mango
— What a tangy taste!

fresh coconut
— sweet and chewy

It's fun to eat things you have made yourself, and your family will like it, too!

21

Glossary

active to be moving, working and doing things

balanced diet a diet made up of different kinds of food

blender a machine for mixing food and making it runny

cereals grains such as rice and oats. Breakfast cereal is also made from them

decay to go bad and rot

diet the food and drink we usually eat

fluid a liquid, such as water or fruit juice

healthy fit and well

inactive sitting or lying still and not moving around much

recipe how to make a dish of food

serving a helping of food

sweat the sticky liquid that comes out of your skin when your body is hot. Sweating helps you to cool down

vitamins substances found in food that help us to stay healthy

Index

Notes
for parents and teachers

- Look through the book and talk about the pictures. Which of the foods do your children like/not like? Are there any foods that your children have not seen or tried before? If so, would they like to try them?

- Foods come in many different colors. Your children could draw a rainbow of different foods. How many red, orange, yellow, green, and blue-violet foods can you think of? Look through cookbooks for inspiration.

- Over a meal, discuss the foods you are eating. Can your children remember how each one helps the body? Is your meal balanced? If not, what would make it so?

- There are many different words to describe the way food looks, tastes, and feels (golden, sweet, slippery, and so on). Make a list of food words with your children. Encourage your children to draw a picture to accompany each word.

- Ask your children to think up a new sandwich for a packed lunch. Together, can you think of a new filling?

- Which are your children's favorite/least favorite foods? You could do a survey of the likes and dislikes of several children. Which foods are the most/least popular?

- Look at the lunch menu at school for a week. Ask your children to say which meals are the healthier choices. Why are the other meals less healthy?

- Have a "Try A New Taste" day. Buy some new foods that your children have never tasted. Display them all and try some. What does each one smell and taste like? Do your children like any of them?

- Do a project on your children's favorite meal. Together, find out which foods it is made from. How and where is the food grown? Help your children to make notes about this.

- What do people in other countries eat for breakfast? Using books and the Internet, find out about breakfasts around the world. How are they different from your usual breakfast? How are they the same?

- Visit the supermarket and look at the labels on fruit and vegetables together to see where the produce was grown.

- Do your children know the alphabet? If they do, play an ABC memory game with different foods, for example: "I went to the store and I bought an apple." "I went to the store and I bought an apple and some bread" etc.

- Using books and the Internet, find out more about how sugar harms our teeth. Help your children to make a factsheet.

> Before undertaking any activity which involves eating, always check whether the children in your care have any food allergies. In a classroom situation, prior written permission from all the parents may be required.